COLOUR OF MY BONES

QASIM KASHMIRI

"THE BOOK DEDICATE MY TO ALL MY READERS"

Contents

Contents

Contents

Preface

Be folishly with me
once you know mw
depart...

..

Foreword

Acknowledgements

Prologue

About The Author

Qasim Kashmiri is the poet and novelist from district Baramulla of north Kashmir. He already has written the books "**Secret OF Dark Night** "and "**The Ashes**". Colour OF My BONES' is his third book which is the collection of poems. He is the great lover of Moulana Rumi as he often writes about his work and continuous to highlight the relationship of readers with Rumi and misreading culture of Rum's work. Qasim is also pursuing PhD in English literature that also helps him to yield interest in reading and writing books.

His poetry is widely read across the country and also has been published in various national and international newspapers and magazines. Many of his poems are translated into Portugal, Persian, polish and German languages. His books are disseminated in **Pakistan, Bangladesh, UK, Poland, and Canada** that heightened the author in many ways.

His novel '**The Ashes'** has been reviewed in various newspapers of the country which succeeded to highlight the issue of inter-caste marriages in Kashmir. The book was much praised my young readers of Kashmir with some noticed flaws.

qkashmir81@gmail.cominstagram: Qasim kashmiri

Author's Note

With a heartfelt gratitude and affection, I strongly express my words of adoration to those who have been reading my poems for all these years and abetted me when I was despondent. Poetry has been my passion and it was more than pain I have been sharing with my readers, but I strongly disagree with those who take poetry just as the part habit but it is rather an ache of living, longing and love.

Poetry for me sounds like sake of or the bottle of poison going deep down in the veins and circulates for hours in unconsciousness. I can't have my exact words to name it or express its true connotation but something that comes senseless yet with all senses, something that torments with sweet pain, and something that takes into skies and throws back to the ground very hard.

I request my readers not to leap into my poems blindly. Please read in complete isolation with the entrance of heart. I don't recommend my lines to those that read them once a place the book on the shelf, just read with inner self or stay away from the book. These are not the words of pride or something but the hand folded request.

Regards!

1. Crystal Bangle

Like a crystal bangle
In a wrist I break
Dying through the ailing moon
Cracking beneath the scorching sun

I am dew on a leaf
A thread of spider's web
Hoops are sinking in the sand
Dusks are failing to take me home

I am lost to be robbed by ants
Ashamed of waiting naked
They hide my August in armpits
Feeding me my rotten flesh

July betrays me every July
Autumn makes me bard
I am murdered by afternoon ants
Chinar is the writer of my death.

2. Rocky Chest

Give me a shield
Or fill my chest with rocks
Wed me with tall ladies
Like those with murky eyes!

Get me a glass of rapt
Hide the wine in armpit
Walk and do not fall till door
We leave the lover who rests.

3. Venom

Inside my void rooms
Silence is dearly wild
Moist papers talk to blood
And the fingers slip away

I have fountains of venom
Pouring out of my bowls
Break the shell of shy and shame
Let some lovers live.

4. Flames

One blow blows a thousand flames
Those thousands give me birth
Else is my tendering self
My heart cannot be sold gladly?

I rock the fire in womb,
Oceans in my lap
Let me bare the colorful bastards
Or burry me in prostitute's grave

Your coming and going is wild
Like a vigor of drifting,
My heels bleed like ugly shepherds
And I breathe out blood for you!

If laila dies for Majnu
And Majnu dies for Laila,
I shall never bemuse my heart
If longs again in scorching deserts.

5. Forbidden fruit

This is now,
A thirst or an ache
Like Adam I relish forbidden fruit!

And
Blister in my throat
Thirst changed its name
A blaze, hell, flame or else!

6. Axe

Take an axe
to my chest
Rocky is my heart
but innocent
My death is written
on the fish hocks
I am yet young to leave!

Come back to me
I am sick
and sold
Scattered brick by brick
My years lost
on the shores
Guilt is my October
I have!

7. Divorced

I shall meet you some day
Beyond the metaphors of farewell
Out of skin and soul
Where existence shall be no more

I shall embrace you some night
In the galaxy of divorced stars,
Through the widow shades of moon
Between the layers of seen and unseen

I shall gild your wrinkled face
With those beads of blood,
All colours shall wish to be red
Mine shall be full of mysteries!

I shall know the stains and grief
That hallucinate me every dusk
My past years shall turn wondrous
And fix my bleeding head and heart.

8. If

If the nights
dress up the lights of sun,
I shall harbor
beside your ugly walls

If your dusk meets mine
I shall forget my bones
like someone forgets umbrella
and passes by

If the wind
blows like last April
or rains like late July,
I shall let my words fall
and fly like October birds

If your presence
mingles up with my solitude,
I shall stay afar
from the excuses of early and late

If my glass fills
and my eyes reflect yours
I shall divorce my wives
and reside with you
till we die together.

9. Die

Cry,
You are the shepherd
In the swift of love

Die,
Be still in the shell
But not broken

Sigh,
And be consumed in love
Like a rain with a smell of mud.

•

10. Drench

Drench with me again
Once more like before;
Your gaze twisted me
Into the widow wails

Your craving gleams me
Like a flash of dawn beam
I am no longer mine to self
Devoured now cell by cell

I behold you in more and less
You fractured me, left wrecked
Call not smith nor carpenter
My cure lies in a dis-ease!

My longing is not ethereal
Not that world is hasty about;
I arise beyond metaphors
Beyond the breath and death

My fasting never ends
I need neither bowls nor barrels
I am thirsty for love
And hungry for beloved.

11. once more

Once more
Like July ants squash beneath
The sole of shoe
I die!

Once more
Like pregnant fish crawls its
Breaths out of ocean
I die!

Once more
Like autumn petals shrivel
And mingle with filth
I die!

Once more
Like a widow woman
Longs for other man
I die!

Once more
Like moths turn to ashes
With the forlorn wink
I die!

Once more
Like fasting beggars
Faint across the doors unknown
I die!

12. Melting Hell

Now senses
are spinning aimlessly
taking me back and forth

Moths roam by night,
every night I resemble them
and making the soulful ardors

His love drizzles the melting hell
shaking fire across my chest
all I desire, one more time!

Begging the bone from Adam;
and the blood from Hawah!
Letting love blast my inward self.

13. Skin and Bone

I lost my way in known
And lost in the unknown,
Aimlessly shattered
Beneath the motherly moon

No longer dressed,
Threw off those worldly
Costumes of skin and bone

Forgotten the names
Those rubbed mine times ago
All my youthful days gone by
Like a horse man passed away

What pain shall I reveal to time?
See, Yusuf cries in one eye
And Zuleikha in the other

I fool the self

Not my unseen beloved!
My love failed at every door
Wandered like a watching-dog.

14. Torment

I drench you along
In this turbulent chase
Long I stood for summers
And called it autumnal love

My longing torments
Every beat of my heartache
I am concealed a bit
More revealed in a drift

Call some other angels,
Let them know this drifting
Izrail, unwillingly busy
Repenting for my blood

Through my dizziness
Through my empty and fullness
World divorced me thrice!
I no longer belong to this mess

His name is only I chant now,
Beating him with seventy hearts
Every beauty is forgotten now
Forgotten my seventy wives

Not day's delight or moment's love
Not fire of hell or paradise green
The room of beggars and lovers
Beyond the more and less.

15. I wonder

Before the breath
Before the death I die
I crave for rebirth
That I never met

In the shadows deep
Half in half out
Rest is unseen
That I never met

Unknown to self
Lost in the known
Other half like quest
That I never met

Seventy fathers ruined
Hundred mothers died
One beloved cried alone
That I never met

They remind, I forget
What to do if senses are lost too
Sobriety chants Allah *hoo*
That I never met.

16. Bones and Flesh

Beyond the bones and flesh
Seventy virgins await;
Witness if ears can see
Pour if eyes can hear

For me I whirl blindly,
Knowing nothing of radiant face
Love means to be sane in insanity
And to be lost in endless surrender!

17. Beggar

My lunacy
roams for sobriety
My migrant soul
devours in abyss,
Perturbing every pulse

Wounding and healing
are the secrets to love
Sewing wounds
by bleeding threads
weave the tales rare

I kiss the shadows
not like that of laila's dog,
Longing through some other way
Bewildered, yet nothing to say

Embrace not in gain
Seek when lost in pain

Love is beggar sometimes
sometimes like a child
Making homes at shoreline,
Let me tell, love is all innocent.

18. Curls

A toxic fragrance lies
Beneath the spell of curls
Ecstasy I call it
And doorway of undying solace

Open the doors and windshields
My ugliness has seventy lovers
World craves for bodily deaths
By threshold, I immortally die

I dream what I lost
Regret the wandering walks
This yearning will never die
It may grieve timelessly

When I heard his music of lips
I beseech the breaths from death
And breathe a few for you
All I claim was beautiful chase

Falling made me stand by
Bowing taught me love,
My nights pass through the moons
Where your face gleams like a wick.

19. Sacred Bath

Send me the holy
waters of pilgrimage
Exile apart my ugly skin
and give me a sacred bath

Through your embraces unlocked
and the palms blocked
I felt the balm venomous
and the saffron colorless

And that ugly widow
who died for years?
to fall in love and betray
with all her bleeding tears

Exile me not anymore
Reckon the hearts you tore
Those fractions won't form a beggar
pick some wolves to bite my remains.

20. Life

This life,
A blink of lusty eyes
One blink through bleeding womb
And other through
The dig beneath

This life,
A deceiving color of peacock,
Sound of moment's nightingale
One time solacing eyes
One time soothing ears…

This life,
A black cloud floating aimlessly
Breaking down into some drops
And endures new form
Then lost into the filth

This life,
A wife of seventy men

And hope of one child
Beautiful for three nights
Ugly for countless moons

This life,
A patch of cloth torn
Small to sleep beneath
Yet with holes
To hide shameful stains

This life,
A child with handful of candies;
Some to lose
Some to eat eagerly
Some to vomit unwillingly

This life
A mystery of union
And painful departure
Less in happiness,
Yet more in pain.

21. Be Still

Collapse by feet, creep by nails
live the sorrows or die
Get me some immortal beloveds
Or teach me the art of leaving!

My treasure resides cosmic
Searching the names erased
Those taste bitter
But sweet to open ears

I circle around the shadows
Beads, deeds then my whisper
Thus doors close and open
Why do the winds blame for?

22. Sell The Beauty

I am not alone
This eye crazes every eye
Sell your beauty and heart
Live there a little more!

You hid your bones behind me
Yet you are patent to my eyes
Does it matter if I seek you?
Fool me not by near and far!

July knows not what December endures
Autumnal winds ever blamed;
The calls call from somewhere,
Where every eye meets you

Now and then the words only,
Words that never engage my lips
Evenings pass through wordless cries
Nights grieve like Milton's Paradise

Don't be veiled for longer,
Merge along where we died
This coming and going is nasty
Let us merge like flawless sun.

23. Not In The Garments

I am yet young to wait
Yet little fool to forget
Bring me some mud
Rebuild my broken self

Be not like a human
Come potent, without veils
I shall call you by the names
By the eyes we shall meet.

24. July Rain

Is this whisper
Or his call?
Why do I press my ears
against the wall?

Some other day
he must visit again
Through the musical
rain drops…

I hunger for you alone
not for breeze or rain

My soul migrates every dusk
Like the July rain drops!
By the dusk I cry out
through the nights I sob
And I marry my silence often
When it speaks everything.

25. Whirlpools

I whirl with whirling whirlpools
Twirling my spinning head
My senses dance devoid of senses
Should not you stay aside?

I drink from empty cups
A rapt of filled barrels
You come to me thirsty
Should not you ask for a sip?

I die in living
And live in dying
My living and dying is one
Should not you ask how?

26. Firewood

Endless times passed
And failed to meet me,
I kiss the cracked cheeks
And sleep with the darkest wine

Love ends up to goose bumps
Teaches to breathe the last
Mystery of my every night
Days I pass with widow smiles

Steals me cell by cell,
One I starved for in youthful days
Thousand times I forgot
Yet millionth times I hunger

My chest sounds like firewood
My sobs louder than thunders
But I waited now and then
Until he artfully drew inside.

27. Hidden

You stayed hidden for sixty years,
Now my seventy bothers not!

A blur turned into blindness
yet you are known to inward me,
Where existence and nonexistence
wonder moon after moon

Give me my ninety,
I shall return your day;
my longing bears no harvest
Exile me apart or take me home!

Let's be broken mirrors,
I shall seek hundreds of you
you may bemuse my eyes
But you will be still you…

I chased my own bones

and my flesh smelt rotten
rotten is my harvest I reaped
I no longer belong to him.

28. My Chest

Who shall die tonight?
Who shall breathe by dawn?
Caravan is thirty at halfway
My chest warbles I say

Half inch sip in throat
Partly drenched, partly quenched
Look back to chasing wolves
My chest warbles I say

Grey is no more grey
Blue is deadly with colorless fetters
Green is now grey, white is now grey
My chest warbles I say

By wrong eyes and right eyes
Brashly with crocodile gestures
Fooling nattily with untied bay
My chest warbles I say

Leap and know this too
Wolf is dressed, man is nude and free
Ignorance is cloaked, innocence to slay
My chest warbles I say

Night was dark and light was bright
Bemused mystery, no longer two
Night is swapping a day
My chest warbles I say.

29. Drum Sticks

Call the my red white
I won't protest,
Turn your ocean into a sip
A thirst will be a thirst

Melody was deadly I heard
But I lost all my drum sticks,
One who hid and appeared apart
Was my childlike secret

Don't press your ear to the walls
Those walls do not respond else
My nails stretch those doors,
Our love is beyond the phrases

Why laila and her face
Why Majnun and his grace?
Beyond my every curtain
There are virgins pink not red

Listen not for pleasure
For pleasure is not always a gift
Love is pain of painful mystery
Where oceans dry up in a drop.

30. Black Bone

Black is my bone
Red is the flesh you relish
Suffocation breathes
Dead is the dowry O moon!

Fire is my neighbour
Living in my rocky chest
Living is beyond the numbers
Death is cure of woe.

31. Be Folish

Be foolishly with me
Once you know me,
Depart,

Gather the bloody baskets
Take me home,
And depart

Gild my ugly face
With eighty veils,
And depart

Come merge again
Live again, love again,
And depart

Tear apart my nails
Or peel out my secrets,
And depart

Give one more body
With a new attire,
And depart

Like a poison be in the glass
Then heal my being,
And depart

Sink deeper yet exiled
Burn our tales,
And depart

Be here, all alone
When I am died,
And depart

Come after you come
Be still when you go
And depart.

32. Embryo

Your dark curls are venomous
Your glance pours the heavens
You exist somewhere in embryo
Perhaps in the candle wick

your eyes let me drift ro sleep
Murmurs drive to rhythms sweet
if I die on the edge of hell
our inion shall be like Adam's mid!

Come along with tenderness
Your arrival is end of all arrivals
You are not from Egyptian vales
But a dream from walnut dye

World fails to define you
You belong to my red poems
If you seed me beneath the filth
How can my soul turn to seventy loves?

33. Kiss The Ground

Ages have nothing to chase
I fall and frisk over the risk
Madly I hit and kiss the ground
Whirling across the doorsills

These coming and going summers
Even the ones those betray halfway
How can I sell my heart
In each vale and every lane?

Come here, stay starved
As you lived hungry since ages
My hunger has thousand tales
And longing is a timeless dis-ease!

Two, three and four bemuse
We hunt mere a drifting soul
Our world is full of toxic drinks,
Offering the colorful barrels of blood

Why your eyes awake before
Before the footfalls and shadows
Stay afar and rub your eyes
Take the flames inside and sleep.

34. Wind-shield

Wind-shield wept
So I crept with rain
There is someone afar;
Someone I never met

I chase my prints
to reach the self
For I know
I buy and sell the secrets

Beyond the cozy evenings
There awaits the poor night
Forget not the carpenter
I dwell in the rich ruins.

35. Thirty Autumns

Hit my chest by drum sticks
I am filled with beast nails
Thirty aitums ruined my cheek,
Sixty mothers fed me venom!

Something I forgot in the way
I met my soil and btought it home
Mystery is not fear if dark nights
I am in war with scorchimng sun.

36. I chase Falling

On every leaf of chinar
I grow and glide away in abyss
Like a forlorn droplet
I chase falling

Between the scenes I cry
And lie behind the bones
I run after the flimsy boats
By the dusk I die

Like a shepherd whooping
Cracking the heels and sigh
I am not a seller from east or west
Or the barks of midnight dogs.

37. A Gift

Throw away the veils
Wrap my shadows as shroud
Autumn is shedding my skin
And the beloved is born red

Not here in my chambers
There is a beast out on threshold
My nails hide the stolen flesh
And I relish it with shepherds

By winds I learn standing
Through the mud I sprout
Beat not the noisy drums
My gift comes from graveyards

They murmur my death in ears
Pressing the foreheads so hard
Regrets won't fetch me back
My bones have ridden by Jhelum.

38. November

Bring me December
Bring me the days forsaken!
Some hands hold pebbles
Some fingers count dead!
I set in grey, grown in green
My tales are written in November!

39. Settle In The Ash

See, in my arms you die like a sick
I yearn to lose every breath too
Like fire of the hell born in my house
I am here to gather the blazes in the palm

The boat has drowned under the waves
I must consume my nights little more
My captain of ship waits for miracle to sail
Not yet young to fall again and be late

This fire is not all like ripe ovaries
This quest is not all I ramble for
My misery is yet to bring virgins from the hell
My rooms are filled with hogs of your vale

I stroll like the flames and settle in the ashes
Send me not the dogs till I reach the door
Bushes and lanes must not confuse my foot
Not should you be hidden like seeds consumed

My rains do not swab my scars or muck
My suns are just the scorching friends of time
Same as the beggar I burst at every door
Where should I go to gather my being?

40. Gross-tops

I wait on gross tops
Like a horizon living afar
Still, silent and sunny

I harvest all dew
A saffron fragrance
And some chinar leaves for you.

41. Because

Because
You did not come
I walked away

Because
You never heard
I kept quiet

Because
You lived afar
I built a wall

Because
You forgot the way
I never looked for abode

Because
You stole my flesh
I put off the frocks

Because
We met again
I forgot the old.

42. Shores

As the night
I am murky and calm
Then wild by the dawn

As the wind
I blow everywhere
Not blowing for long

As the wax
The flames torment me
A tale of my every bone

As the fire
I consume the dry
Full of melting desires

As the boat
I sail with the holes
Searching the distant shores.

43. Friendly Winds

I carry
My heart in my fist
Roaming
with the shepherds;

Fill me with hope
My ship has drowned
so deep;

Sell me
not to unknown roamers,
I long
to stay for friendly winds;

Ask my bones not the flesh
The secrets of death lie
in my letters!

44. I Know

I know
The wind is blurry
The way is bushy till the pole
Come across, ten heels more

Don't reckon the older days
The winter stayed so long
My letters are wet and wasted
Waiting for the august sun

See the dust is up
Why do we not rise along?
Hit my door enter by knees
Your brow is full of sorrows

My face is older
Older is my heart
Nights are dark and dull
Send me some suns to sheen
You often ramble and reel

In the chill of my dusks
Smiles and laughs die together
Do not hide your cheeks

We are here to pass by
Smile, surrender, cry and die
You wish to long again
You wish to stay I know.

45. Twice

My I is yours
Your you is mine,
We swap the souls
Not these mortal covers

Two is hard to be
One is all to be,
These numbers just echoes
Beyond is a gift of love!

A gift is not corporal,
Nor an object of eye
Go in the layers deep
The shores are not the ends!

Fooling is a skill if beautiful
Sanity always is not a victory
If you gamble once or twice
You postpone the endless love

Beyond everything we lose
How hard to embrace it!
How beautiful it would be
If we live twice!

46. speck

Walk with me, sit with agony
Our tales resemble O friend
Where else to wander?
Be here to collect the wrecks

Speck is my master of forehead
My tongue has scars of poison
Grief taught me to sit aside
Living is a camel's walk

Before I burn I burn
I rise again to fall gain
My rising is a circle of butterflies
Light, little and low

Like a rock or a rambling cloud
I am still and swift aftermath
My tale is a seed of ache
I am the smith of my shell.

47. I Am

I am
Where the candle blows
And night meets the grief

I am
Where the moon sobs
In the arms of child

I am
Where the lovers meet,
Carrying hearts in their fist

I am
Where the letters float
Upon the waters of eyes

I am
Where widows hoot
Under the veils of seventy men

I am
Where death wears up
And life nakedly wanders.

48. Quest

Let's forget the hog
Forgive the bushes
All those camels too

Far in those deserts
Lies a beautiful quest
Half mine and half yours

Beyond that we lark but late
Share the pebbles and rain
And sleep with the sand

And just after a line
There is a festival my friend,
Selling our loves there

Seed in my fist
And mud in your armpits
Growing the moans my friend

Come, let's learn to love
Like we never born humans
Live like we don't know dying.

49. A Gaze

A gaze across the gaze
where the hope hopes
sighing, dying, crying
Hoot after hoot
As longing of saffron girls
Tossing the pearls of love
What name for this love
why should call it else?
Love is not revealed
Nor concealed between the two!

50. Robbed My Attires

My tales go with the flames
With the wick and the smoke
Wisp by wisp I whirl in circles
Settling down in the wicked odor
Zealously in the mist we meet
Like a wind with the burned
Under the yellow scars of sky
I wait, darting the end of pole!

And with the saffron threads
Out in the field we draw together
Those girls with cracked cheeks
Gather my baskets and run!
Beauty robbed my attires,
Ugliness ran away with Majnuns
I sing the naked pains in the deserts
Traveling with pregnant camels.

51. Love is Ahead

Inside the core of ach, don't ran away
Be on the shores and meet the beloved
Tearing frocks is an old excuse now
All rumours of beloved not often true

Love is ahead, calling exquisitely
And the clouds soon wane away
Beyond everything we will sail across
Call your beloved and let me call mine

This gamble of the blood is an escape
We are the little souls to play aside
Not all who went lived eternal there
Be holy and sail along with innocence

Meet the rapt and don't come back
Live there the rest, you are so exhausted
Before the master comes be there on the sill
Love when the world comes to you as falcon.

52. Not So Open

Do not enter the room of love
The beloved is not sold so open
What else his face there would be
Bemusing is a game of loss

The way long walking and him
The hanger and the pots broken
All I carried was petty and ugly
Shall I wait there for one more time?

Forget bargaining, buy a few pots more
Carry my head, seventy houses to go
My hunger is not like others have
Does it bother if protest for bowls too?

My love tales are not sweet
Not full of gifts O sun
An age or an eternal chase
But we are near like eye to eye!

I sit before the fire and cry
It sounds my cries I hear
We join the heads like grass-tops
Cry in silence and die with brash.

53. Pink smiles

Be with me like eye to eye
Like brick to brick on the wall
Let's slowly talk to each other
Like a healer with a sick!

I have been waiting here
Since we met beyond the unseen
Why do these miles craze still?
Take a hammer to the walls

I am still young with plump cheeks
My face is full of pink smiles
I do not count the men anymore
Come; be together in the swift of love

Why you fled too early before the sun
See, my compound is full of bruises
I have one more garden in the backyard
No one shall ever relish it but you

Your lips will hold my flute
And I shall hear on the sills
On the walnut chairs we will rock
By the evening we shall drink with the stars

Don't yell, we wept last night
Just for a little life we lost
Why do not steal a few moments
Be there without more and less

Back to the sleep I croon all night
My love is louder, having no choice
My neighbours pelt the stones often
And Count with a sheer laughter

Mad I am in the realm of giving
Sold everything, nothing for the self
Send me the harvest of my love
I have been bagger for all these years.

54. Questions

Wet in the fresh droplets,
the rain slid away through me

our kisses were postponed,
windshield took me back

By those touches I healed up,
sipped in his cups and screamed

tossed and set my heart on fire,
burning saved me from the chill

then after the years it happened,
my child born from the mud

I assaulted the self by the questions,
silence answered all the rumours.

55. A drift

A drift
or a spinning rock
some venom, inside

Death of unknown
never met ruins
a caravan of numb, inside

Nowhere here
not even behind
a mirror broken, inside

Shades, not shadows
cry of wounded lambs
pain of shepherd, inside

Basket of saffron
handful of dusts
a seller of scrubs, inside

Trodden not trembled
tears, not the rain drops
a festival of fire, inside

Marriage of nightingale
Peacocks ashamed of black legs
A wail of virgin, inside

Bowls filled with honey,
serpents gilded on a sip
the holes unseen, inside.

56. Take Me Home

Take me home, now the day is gone
Shepherd is back with sheep and song
Wolves roar there and still afar
Hold my hand before they reach

Wind is heavy and clouds burst
Fresh is not a prey but my flesh is
Turn back and tell your horse
We were together when we came

Should I pay the bread or what?
Why these prices if you agreed at home
I shall complaint to mothers who wait
You are so tough, do not trait

My roosters are dark I know the colours
My sheep are thirty I know their fur
Don't assure me with all these numbers
The wolf was far, near we stayed.

57. Dearly Flames

A flame in my inward self
Is my heartache o friend
You burn with wax and wick
I melt with dearly flames

Follow not my prints
Stay alone or exiled
I am robbed my termites
I have forgotten the way

I am his shadow inside and out
My fractions devour me pore by pore
Drifting my soul through love phrases
I am sane with pretty checkmate.

58. Nodding

A call,
whisper,
and a breath

blasting me
death by death

I surrender my wish
By nodding!

I am the widow of seventy men.

59. who

Who held these words without me?
Who filled your ears with rumours?
My blood made the lanes and beads
The skin stitched into garments
My doors are not shut
Walls are still half built
The house is empty but serene
Awaking with all night tavern

Who else dinned the days with you?
Recall, we walked hand in hand
We hugged the butterflies together
And played with the paper boats

Those storms not mine not yours
Bags we forgot are full of moons
Someone betrayed and we ran dismay
Someday we shall visit again
Again in the cow dung circles
We shall meet with walnut dye
The bushes will recognise us

Like the grasshoppers or dew

And will not die there this summer.

60. Necklace

I am the necklace
around your neck
Hold on this exaltation,
be not ugly in the crowd

My beads sheen in your eyes
forget blindfold, look into my eyes
I am seller of costumes and veils
your beauty is my debt, they know

Empty my hands, I carry by eyes
confusions should not exist any more
We are clear like the crystal droplets
tumbling artfully on each other

Poetry does not reach but my eyes do
two camels need not to gallop slowly
I am walking by foot through scrubs
before I roam elsewhere, rush toward me.

61. Leaves

Back in my vales
A song with a howl
Sweet for a little
Bitter for the ages
Lost in the pursuit
Blinded void folds
Run the fingers on my chest
Give some name to illness

If I sell my heart for a pitcher
You will fall in love and loss
Living and dying making us laugh
Else is just a grave of leaves
Your face is still splendour
Those eyes are still full of zest
I know the forgetting is hard
Let not your heart be master.

62. I Shall Wait

I shall wait
Till the miracle happens
When all glory arrives
And rests in your clinch

I shall wait
Till the caravan comes back
And grazes again
Through the green graves

I shall wait
Till the remarriage of souls
When I will be like you
And you will be like me

I shall wait
Till I meet my angel of death
When he will trap me
And I will torment him back

I shall wait
Till my rival sits on a pillow
When I offer him my tears
And he will wipe and cry

I shall wait
Till my wives are back
When hands full of wine
And I shall rest in their arms

I shall wait
Till my faces turn beautiful
When my cheeks look younger
Then attract many men

I shall wait
Till the sun blaze again
When the moon bursts on shoulders
And I shall squeeze both

I shall wait
Till I live again with me

When I shall build again my bones
and learn to love the self.

63. Charcoal Face

And a crystal heart fell away
Strewn into the debris
Each mirrored my charcoal face

I need the seventy wives
Few bangles and some gowns
My April is yet to come

Look at me through the holes
I am beautiful if seen
No matter on the sooty floor

Rub your dust and sit
Fold the hands so humbly
Beg the shepherd some fleece.

The End

Tearing frocks is old excuse

    Rumors are not always true

www.ingramcontent.com/pod-product-compliance
Ingram Content Group UK Ltd.
Pitfield, Milton Keynes, MK11 3LW, UK
UKHW011343160826
14477UKWH00022B/225

9 798886 297256